Let's Stretch!

by Sarah Snashall

illustrated by Helen Morgan

Wake up!

Are you a runner or a swimmer? Are you a footballer on the football pitch?

What should you do when you want to play sport?

You should wake up your body! If you start too fast, you might get a stitch.

You need to prepare your body to do sport.

You can stretch and do short **drills**.

1 We get our legs ready to run.

2 We get our arms ready to catch.

3 We get our shoulders ready to bat.

Get Ready for Football

She wakes up her legs. First, she marches on the spot. Then she runs between the cones.

He hops over the ladder. His feet are fast!

He passes the ball.

Get Ready to Twirl

There are many ways to stretch.

He wants to leap and twirl. He can reach further after he stretches.

He points one leg out behind him.

Then he switches legs.

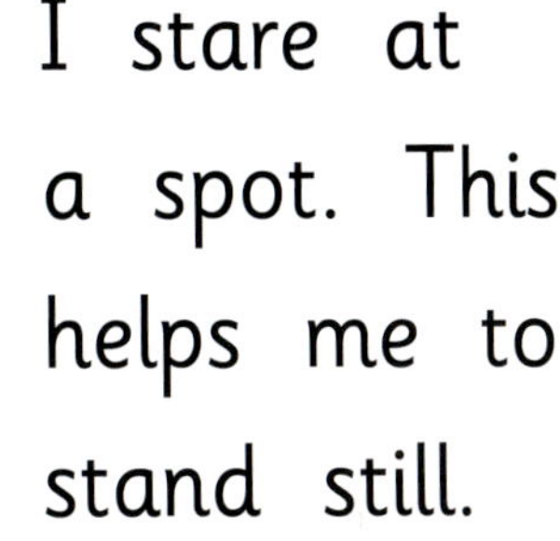

Get Ready to Swim

She gets her body ready to swim. First, she splashes her legs. The water is chilly!

He is ready to swim!

Get Ready for Tennis

He wants to stretch his shoulders. He holds one arm across his body. Then he will switch arms.

She has already stretched her arms. Now she can hit the ball.

Get Ready to Skate

She wears skates to twist and turn on the ice. First, she will stretch her legs.

Her friend stretches on the ice. She lifts one leg up. Then she swaps legs.

Now they are both ready to skate!

Get Ready for Gymnastics

She is getting ready to do gymnastics.
She stretches her leg to the side. Her mum stretches, too!

I sit like this to stretch my **hips**.

He has stretched already. Now he can **flip** and spin.

Stretch again!

The match has finished. These players are the winners!

They celebrate after the match. Then they will stretch again.

After sport, we should stretch each part of our body.

If we don't stretch, our bodies might hurt.

Stretch for Fun

They stretch to relax. They wear stretchy clothes. They have bare feet.

There are lots of stretches you can do.
These stretches look like animals ...

Stretch with Friends

These children share a stretch. They stand and hold hands. They take care not to pull too hard.

Now it is time to rest. These children lie down where they are.

Glossary

cobra: a kind of snake

drills: short activities you do to train for sport

flip: to turn over quickly

hips: the bony parts at the side of your body between your legs and tummy

Index